S0-CFN-681

Golden State
WARRIORS

BY K.C. KELLEY

The Child's World®
childsworld.com

Published by The Child's World®
1980 Lookout Drive • Mankato, MN 56003-1705
800-599-READ • www.childsworld.com

ISBN 9781503824607
LCCN 2018964277

Printed in the United States of America
PA02416

ABOUT THE AUTHOR

K.C. Kelley is a huge sports fan who has
written more than 150 books for kids.
He has written about football, basketball,
soccer, and even auto racing! He lives in
Santa Barbara, California.

TABLE OF

CONTENTS

GO, WARRIORS!

The Golden State Warriors' trophy case is getting crowded. Since 2015, they have won three NBA titles. Along the way, they have thrilled their fans. The team plays with speed and great spirit. The Warriors are the biggest news in the NBA. Let's meet the Golden State Warriors!

Superstar Stephen Curry has helped turn today's Warriors into an NBA champion.

All-Star Kevin Durant goes to the hoop in a Western Conference game against the Lakers.

WHO ARE THE WARRIORS?

The Warriors are one of 30 NBA teams. The Warriors play in the Pacific Division of the Western Conference. The other Pacific Division teams are the Los Angeles Clippers, the Los Angeles Lakers, the Phoenix Suns, and the Sacramento Kings. The Warriors have tough battles with their Pacific Division **rivals**!

WHERE THEY CAME FROM

The Warriors began in 1946 in the Basketball Association of America (BAA). The team first played in Philadelphia. In 1949, BAA teams joined the NBA. In 1962, the Warriors moved to San Francisco. Starting with the 1971–72 season, the team changed its name to the Golden State Warriors. California is nicknamed the Golden State.

Among the nicknames for the Warriors' Wilt Chamberlain? The Big Dipper and Wilt the Stilt.

Sweet shooting by Klay Thompson has been a big reason for the Warriors' success.

WHO THEY PLAY

The Warriors play 82 games each season. They play 41 games at home and 41 on the road. The Warriors play four games against each of the other Pacific Division teams. They play 36 games against other Western Conference teams. The Warriors also play each of the teams in the Eastern Conference twice. That's a lot of basketball! Each June, the winners of the Western and Eastern Conferences play each other in the NBA Finals.

WHERE THEY PLAY

The Warriors moved into a brand-new home for the 2019–20 NBA season. The team spent $1 billion on their new arena, called the Chase Center. The building is in San Francisco. From 1971 to 2018, the Warriors played at the Oracle Arena in Oakland. Until the Warriors left, it was the oldest arena in the league.

By the time you read this, the Warriors will be playing inside this brand-new arena in San Francisco.

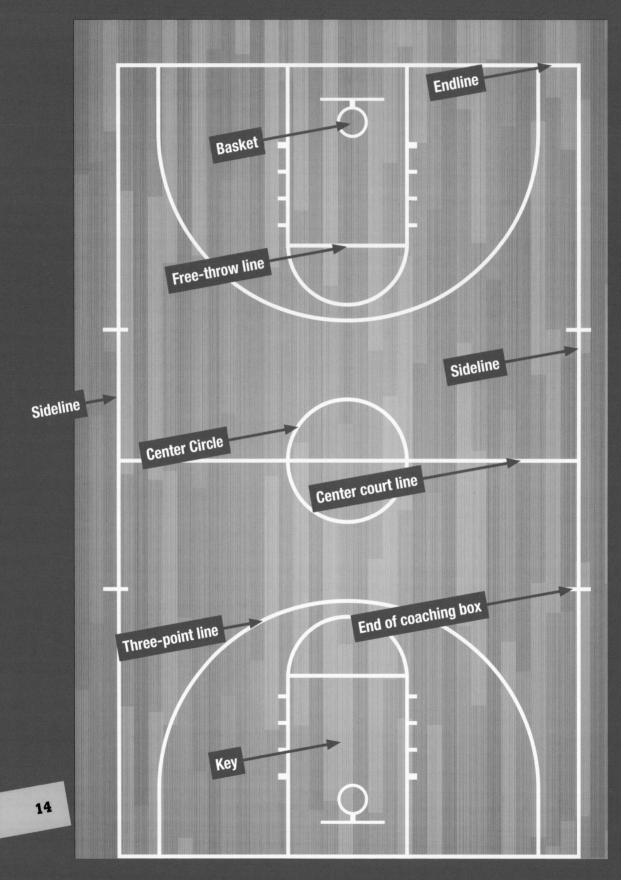

THE BASKETBALL COURT

An NBA court is 94 feet long and 50 feet wide (28.6 m by 15.24 m). Nearly all the courts are made from hard maple wood. Rubber mats under the wood help make the floor springy. Each team paints the court with its logo and colors. Lines on the court show the players where to take shots. The diagram on the left shows the important parts of the NBA court.

The Warriors' new home will have 19 escalators. The team president says that is a record for an NBA arena!

GOOD TIMES

The first season of the Basketball Association of America was 1946–47. The Philadelphia Warriors were the BAA's first champion. As the Golden State Warriors, the team was the 1975 NBA champion. The Warriors also reached the **NBA Finals** every season from 2014–15 to 2018-19. They won the NBA title in 2015, 2017, and 2018. In the 2015–16 season, they set an NBA record with 73 wins.

Another title, another parade! Stephen Curry shows fans the 2018 NBA championship trophy.

During a tough 2000–01 season, Golden State's Antawn Jamison had this shot blocked!

TOUGH TIMES

When the Warriors were in Philadelphia, their worst season was 1952–53. They won only 12 games! The Warriors' had a bad stretch from 1994 through 2006. In those seasons, Golden State never had a winning record. In the 2000–01 season, the Warriors set a team record with 65 losses.

ALL THE RIGHT MOVES

Warriors **guard** Stephen Curry is probably the best ever at **three-point shots**. He practices shooting for many hours. The hard work pays off. He can make long shots from almost anywhere. Teammate Klay Thompson is almost as good. Thompson set a single-game NBA record in 2018 with 14 three-point baskets.

Basketball has not always had a three-point shot. The NBA didn't add it until 1979.

This is the shooting form that has made Stephen Curry the best ever at making three-pointers.

In 1962, Wilt Chamberlain became the only NBA player to score 100 points in a game.

HEROES THEN

Paul Arizin was one of the NBA's early shooting stars. He played 10 seasons with the Warriors and twice led the NBA in scoring. Wilt "The Stilt" Chamberlain was one of the best players of all time. In one season, he averaged an amazing 50.4 points per game! He also led the NBA in **rebounding** 11 times. Guard Rick Barry was a great shooter and **dribbler**. He took free-throw shots underhanded.

HEROES NOW

Stephen Curry turned the Warriors into a championship team. He is a great passer and outstanding shooter. Curry and Klay Thompson are called the "Splash Brothers." Their long-range shots "splash" into the basket. Kevin Durant plays **forward**. He is an outstanding scorer and plays great defense. Draymond Green works hard for rebounds and **inspires** his teammates.

Draymond Green brings championship energy to the Warriors. He's also a top rebounder.

WHAT THEY WEAR

NBA players wear a **tank top** jersey. Players wear team shorts. Each player can choose his own sneakers. Some players also wear knee pads or wrist guards.

Each NBA team has more than one jersey style. The pictures at left show some of the Warriors' jerseys.

The NBA basketball (left) is 29.5 inches (75 cm) around. It is covered with leather. The leather has small bumps called pebbles.

The pebbles on a basketball help players grip it.

TEAM STATS

Here are some of the all-time career records for the Golden State Warriors. These stats are complete through all of the 2018–19 NBA regular season.

THREE-POINTERS

Stephen Curry	2,483
Klay Thompson	1,798

POINTS PER GAME

Wilt Chamberlain	41.5
Kevin Durant	25.8

ASSISTS PER GAME

Tim Hardaway	9.3
Guy Rodgers	8.3

REBOUNDS PER GAME

Wilt Chamberlain	25.1
Nate Thurmond	16.9

STEALS PER GAME

Rick Barry	2.3
Baron Davis	2.0

FREE-THROW PCT.

Stephen Curry	.905
Rick Barry	.896

GAMES	
Chris Mullin	807
Nate Thurmond	757

CHRIS MULLIN

29

GLOSSARY

assists *(uh-SISTS)* passes that lead directly to a basket

dribbler *(DRIB-ler)* a player who is moving the ball up the court by bouncing it over and over

forward *(FORE-word)* a player in basketball who usually plays away from the basket

guard *(GARD)* a player in basketball who usually dribbles and makes passes

inspires *(in-SPYRES)* creates a desire to succeed

NBA Finals *(NBA FINE-ulz)* the championship series for the NBA

rebounding *(REE-bownd-ing)* the act of grabbing or picking up a missed shot at the basket

rivals *(RY-vuhlz)* two people or groups competing for the same thing

tank top *(TANK TOP)* a style of shirt that has straps over the shoulders and no sleeves

three-point shot *(THREE-poynt SHOT)* a basket worth three points that is made from outside a curved line on the court

FIND OUT MORE

IN THE LIBRARY

Fishman, Jon. M. *Basketball Superstars: Stephen Curry.* Minneapolis, MN: Lerner Classroom, 2019.

Goodman, Michael E. *NBA Champions: Golden State Warriors.* Mankato, MN: Creative Paperbacks, 2018.

Sports Illustrated Kids (editors). *Big Book of Who: Basketball.* New York: Sports Illustrated Kids, 2015.

ON THE WEB

Visit our website for links about the Golden State Warriors:
childsworld.com/links

Note to Parents, Teachers, and Librarians: We routinely verify our Web links to make sure they are safe and active sites. So encourage your readers to check them out!

INDEX